SAIL
William Fish Williams's Story

told by Michael Sandler
illustrated by Bert Dodson

SCHOOL PUBLISHERS

Cover, ©Alain Nogues/CORBIS SYGMA; p.3, ©Buddy Mays/CORBIS; p.7, ©Roy Toft/National Geographic/Getty Images; p.8, ©Konrad Wothe/Minden Pictures; p.9, ©Hiroya Minakuchi/Minden Picture; p.10,©The Art Archive/Naval Museum Genoa/Dagli Orti; p.11, ©SSPL/The Image Works; p.14, ©The Art Archive/Culver Pictures.

Copyright © by Harcourt, Inc.

All rights reserved. No part of this publication may be reproduced or transmitted in any form or by any means, electronic or mechanical, including photocopy, recording, or any information storage and retrieval system, without permission in writing from the publisher.

Requests for permission to make copies of any part of the work should be addressed to School Permissions and Copyrights, Harcourt, Inc., 6277 Sea Harbor Drive, Orlando, Florida 32887–6777. Fax: 407-345-2418.

HARCOURT and the Harcourt Logo are trademarks of Harcourt, Inc., registered in the United States of America and/or other jurisdictions.

Printed in China

ISBN 10: 0-15-351030-7
ISBN 13: 978-0-15-351030-4

Ordering Options
ISBN 10: 0-15-350602-4 (Grade 5 On-Level Collection)
ISBN 13: 978-0-15-350602-4 (Grade 5 On-Level Collection)
ISBN 10: 0-15-357955-2 (package of 5)
ISBN 13: 978-0-15-357955-4 (package of 5)

If you have received these materials as examination copies free of charge, Harcourt School Publishers retains title to the materials and they may not be resold. Resale of examination copies is strictly prohibited and is illegal.

Possession of this publication in print format does not entitle users to convert this publication, or any portion of it, into electronic format.

5 6 7 8 9 10 468 12 11 10 09

Born at Sea

Some people are born in the country. Others are born in the city. I was born in neither place. I came into this world in the middle of the ocean.

My father, Thomas Williams, a ship's captain, seldom spent much time on land. My mother, Eliza, traveled the seven seas with him. On January 12, 1859, while my father's ship, the *Florida*, was sailing in the Tasman Sea off of Australia, I was born.

The voyages my father took were long. At the time of my birth, the *Florida* was just beginning a three-year journey. For this reason, all my earliest memories are of the sea.

When I think of my childhood, I see seagulls perched on a mast. I smell the fresh salty scent of the ocean. I hear the sound of sails flapping in the wind.

I know that I grew up differently from many children. Most children learn to walk on sidewalks or grassy fields. My first steps were taken on the wooden planks of a ship's deck. Most children learn to fall asleep with a mother's hand rocking the cradle. For me, the gentle motion of the waves sent me into my dreams. In some ways, however, my early days were similar to those of other children.

I grew up surrounded by family. In addition to my mother and father, I had two uncles aboard the ship. There were also my two older brothers, Thomas and Henry. Eventually, my sister, Mary, joined us. She was born during the same trip, two years after me.

I even had a pet, the ship's cat. It ran around the ship chasing after mice. I ran around the ship chasing after it.

In fact, the whole ship was a playground during that first voyage. I tumbled around the deck. I climbed over boxes and chains. I played hide-and-seek behind oak barrels.

Sometimes when the sea was rough, I'd trip and sprawl. A sailor would scoop me up and carry me into the cabin. There my mother was waiting to wipe away my tears.

Of course, I had to stay out of the way while the sailors conducted their chores. They were busy from morning until night. They began each day by washing down the decks. First, they filled buckets of water from a tub. Then, they poured the water out onto the planks and carefully swept them with brooms. They used mops to soak up any leftover water. My father would come by to make sure everything was dry and clean. He liked his ship to be spotless!

Creatures of the Sea

Children growing up on land learn about life around them. They learn to recognize different kinds of dogs. They learn the names of flowers and bushes. They can tell the difference between types of trees.

I rarely saw a dog or a tree—only when the ship was in port. I could tell you everything, however, about the creatures of the sea. I learned about the fish, the mammals, and the birds. I could tell a Cape Horn pigeon from an ordinary gull by the way it fluttered just above the waves. I knew a fish called a sawshark by its long toothed snout. I knew dozens of types of squid.

What I looked forward to most were the whales. Someone would spot the wispy plume of water that spouted from a whale when it broke the surface of the sea. Then everyone would come on deck to see the great creatures.

I learned the names of all the different types of whales. I knew a sperm whale by its huge head. I recognized the wrinkled skin on its back. This set it apart from other large whales. Most have very smooth skin.

An orca surfacing

Sperm whale

    I could tell a right whale by its long droopy mouth and the lack of a dorsal fin. There were so many different kinds of whales! Some whales seemed as long as the ship. I would stare down at them over the rail. The sight filled me with fear. Their mouths were so huge! Their tails were so strong! I worried that they might strike the ship and shatter its hull.

Danger at Sea

In truth, getting sunk by a whale wasn't likely. Sailing, however, was a risky business. As I grew older, I began to understand the real dangers that we faced.

Storms were chief among them. Typhoons were common in the Pacific Ocean. Winds tore at the sails and whipped up the waves. Our boat would shiver and shake. I remember one storm with waves so high that I felt sure the ship would broach. My father saw my nervous face. He tried to calm me down.

"Remember who is steering this ship, Willie," he laughed. "No storm has beaten your father yet."

Yes, my father could handle nature's fury. It was human error that filled him with fear. Fire was his chief concern.

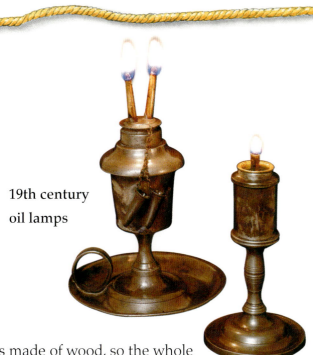

19th century oil lamps

The ship was made of wood, so the whole boat was highly inflammable. Everything could burn. If the ship did catch fire, there was nowhere to escape. My father always warned the crew to be careful with candles, matches, stoves, and oil.

"Don't burn down our home," he would say, smiling but deadly serious.

Becoming a Sailor

In between voyages, I spent several periods living on land. Friends would ask me about life at sea. "Don't you get bored?" they'd ask. "Don't you long to come back to shore?"

"Never," I'd reply. It was true. Life on land seemed dull compared to life on a ship.

   While I was on land, I missed the sea and its creatures. I missed the adventure. I missed the songs of the rowdy sailors. No two days at sea were ever the same. There was always something to see. There was always something to do.

   As I grew into my teens, my days aboard the ship were filled with learning. I was learning how to be a sailor. I studied how to coil the ropes, and I practiced tying the knots. I put aside fear and learned how to climb the masts. I became skilled at handling oars. With each passing voyage, I grew more and more able.

A Day to Remember

My fondest memory is of December 25, 1873. I was fifteen years old. Our family was headed out on a new ship, the *Florence*. It was the very first day of the trip.

For this voyage, my role had changed. Now I wasn't just a captain's son. This was my very first day as an "official" member of the crew. As the *Florence* sailed away from San Francisco, I was filled with joy. Though I didn't know it, the best was yet to come.

The *Florence* carried four small boats. These were used for special expeditions away from the large ship. Each carried a four-man crew. Crews would stay the same for the entire journey.

A few hours into our trip, my father called the crew together. He and three officers were going to choose the sailors who would go with them when the small boats were lowered into the water.

I took my place with the other sailors. I had no hope of being picked, but I felt dignified just to be standing with the group. The crews were selected one by one. Then it was my father's turn to pick his third and final sailor. I nearly fell over when I heard his words.

"I will take my boy," he said.

I had never felt so proud in my life. At last, I had become a true sailor!

A 19th century sea captain

Think Critically

1. Where and when does the narrator's tale begin?

2. Compare the narrator's early life to that of other children. How are they alike? How are they different?

3. What part of the book did you find the most interesting?

4. Why was the narrator surprised by his father's action at the end of the story?

5. Is this story told from the first-person or third-person point of view? How do you know?

 Social Studies

Explore San Francisco San Francisco is mentioned in this story. Use the Internet or other library resource to learn more about the city of San Francisco. Where is it located? What are some important events that occurred in San Francisco? Summarize your findings.

School-Home Connection Share the ending of the book with family members. Then compare William's experience with moments from your own lives when you felt especially proud.

Word Count: 1,297